'Imagination is not fantasy. In these meditations Rhidian Brook invites us to fire our own imagination as we try to "live" through that week. We are left with the questions: who is Jesus? And: where do I stand in these scenarios?'
Nick Baines, Bishop of Leeds and author of *Who Am I?*

'Rhidian Brook tells the story of Holy Week as you have never heard it before. He draws you into the inner life of the first followers of Jesus, reclaims Christianity as an adventure of the spirit, and brings the whole thing alive again. He is a master storyteller re-narrating the greatest story ever told.'
Giles Fraser, vicar, broadcaster and author of *Chosen: Lost and found between Christianity and Judaism*

'In a contemporary informal style this eyewitness account invites the reader to walk with Jesus in his last days and experience anew the power of his resurrection. A vivid retelling which brings fresh life to a familiar story.'
Richard Harries, former Bishop of Oxford and author of *Hearing God in Poetry*

'As one who resides near the Old City in Jerusalem, I have had the privilege of witnessing countless pilgrims as they journey through these sacred streets, seeking to touch the very ground where our Lord walked. It was during his own time among us that I came to know Rhidian Brook. His profound curiosity and reverence for the historical weight of this Holy City were evident, and it is this same spirit that imbues his remarkable book, *Notes on an Execution*. Rhidian's reflections offer a unique and deeply personal lens through which to experience the tumultuous final days of Jesus. By inviting us to "unknow what we know", he masterfully empowers his readers to walk alongside the disciples, feeling the bewilderment, the hope and the eventual sorrow and joy as events unfold. This book is not merely a recounting; it is an invitation to inhabit the story, making it a vital companion for anyone seeking a more immediate and heartfelt understanding of Christ's passion and resurrection.'

The Most Revd Dr Hosam E. Naoum, Anglican Archbishop in Jerusalem

'Understated, loaded and awful. I love this little book. Rhidian makes us followers of Jesus as he walks towards the end of his mortal life. Glimpses of glory and favour, of impending danger, of wonderful women, of the cringeworthy casting off of cultural norms. Then confounding wisdom and snatches of his last words. All this, and no understanding at all of the day he changed the world or why he deliberately went for it.'

Jackie Pullinger, founder of the St Stephen's Society and author of *Chasing the Dragon*

'Rhidian Brook writes with such understanding of the human condition about the Saviour who is both human and God. We find ourselves written into this universal story, and there are questions which must be answered. This interpretation of the Passion opens up new vistas of the soul's journey through life towards death.'

Richard Sewell, Dean of St George's Cathedral, Jerusalem

'With deft insight and lightness of touch Rhidian Brook lifts the Holy Week story from the reverence of the gospels and the solemnity of liturgy into direct and lively accounts of genuine interaction and moving encounter. This is an ideal account for a newcomer and a refreshing repristination for the over-familiar.'

Sam Wells, vicar, broadcaster and author of *Constructing an Incarnational Theology*

Rhidian Brook is an award-winning writer of fiction, television drama and film. His first novel, *The Testimony of Taliesin Jones* (1996), won several prizes, including the Somerset Maugham Award. His third novel, *The Aftermath* (2013), was an international bestseller, translated into twenty-five languages and made into a film starring Keira Knightley. He wrote an original screenplay for the BBC drama, *Mr Harvey Lights A Candle*, starring Timothy Spall; was a writer on two seasons of *Silent Witness*; and wrote the original screenplay of the film *Africa United*. He has adapted his most recent novel – *The Killing of Butterfly Joe* (2018) – for film. He has been a regular contributor to BBC Radio 4's 'Thought for the Day' for twenty-five years. A collection of his 'Thoughts', entitled *Godbothering*, was published in 2020. He is currently writing a novel inspired by the year he spent living in Jerusalem.

For my mother, Vanessa

Notes on an Execution

Rhidian Brook

Lenten reflections
on the last days of Jesus

spck

Contents

Foreword

Every three years, churches across the Western world re-encounter the abrupt and breathless account that is the Gospel according to Mark. Considerably shorter than the other three renderings of Jesus' life in the New Testament, Mark offers us a deeply human Jesus, seized with the urgency of his mission, and consistently misunderstood by his followers.

It is not always easy to connect with this particular Jesus, for we live some two thousand years on what Rhidian Brook calls the 'far side of his story', our minds awash with an amalgam of the four Gospels, and layers of accrued piety. But for the seven days of Holy Week, 2024, congregations in York Minster found themselves on the edge of their seats, drawn once again into Mark's compelling and demanding drama, as if we, ourselves, were onlookers and disciples in the extraordinary events of that unique week.

Part meditation, part sermon, part news report, part poetry, and fully Rhidian Brook at his most focused and evocative, these Notes are an arresting and courageous refocusing of our lens on to – and into – the urgent and bewildering climax of what Mark tells his readers (at the very beginning of his brief work) is 'The good news of Jesus Christ'. As you read these pages, I hope that, like those of us in York Minster in the Holy Week of 2024, you may also discover the truth of Mark's great claim, brought alive for us afresh in this disconcerting and powerful narrative.

The Very Reverend Dominic Barrington
Dean of York

Preface

This little book was conceived in Jerusalem and delivered in York.

I was living in Jerusalem when the new Dean of York, Dominic Barrington, asked if I would be willing to deliver the Holy Week sermons at the Minster for 2024. Without knowing what this might entail, I said yes. After all, I was in the very place where the events – now celebrated and remembered at Holy Week – actually happened. I was literally treading in the footsteps of Jesus on my way to work every morning. The Via Dolorosa was part of my daily commute.

Living in Jerusalem brought home the everyday aspect of the gospel stories and the fact that the events they describe have unavoidable particularity. I often found myself speculating as to what it would have been like to witness the last days of Jesus in real time. How would I have reacted had I been there?

That Palm Sunday celebration in 2023 saw around five thousand people walk from Bethany via Gethsemane to the Pools of Bethesda. It was a scene of joy, and easy to imagine being there, at that first triumphal entry with Jesus somewhere up ahead, riding into the city that, a week later, would kill him.

The story of the death of a man called Jesus in a remote part of the Roman Empire has a particular geography in Jerusalem. And while we can argue as to exactly where

X marks the spot, we know that it happened and that it happened there. It is possibly the most told and retold story on earth and yet it still bears the weight of its own familiarity. How to tell it again? How to see the story anew and help others do the same?

I decided to go with those feelings and impressions I had experienced on that Palm Sunday march down the Mount of Olives and in my amblings in and around the Old City. To take the point of view of the ones following Jesus in those last days, and to 'see' events as a collective third person, observing them from another angle, as though through the lens of a handheld camera, where what we see is sometimes in close up and in sharp focus, and then suddenly blurred, bewildering and hard to comprehend.

I wanted to try and imagine what it was like for those followers, not knowing what was going to happen next, and feeling joyous, hapless, helpless and afraid. To create a sense of witnessing these events for the first time, this side of history and this side of his story, without the theology or exegesis that came later (as much as is possible given the sources were all written wise-after-the-event!).

This book follows Jesus from his arrival in Bethany through to his last moments on the cross. Of the four Gospels, Mark gives perhaps the best sense of the day to day, and I have leant in on Mark's account for the bulk of my own reimagining of the week, drawing on John for the detail of the execution and Luke for the encounter with the risen Jesus.

The resurrection also has a geography; it is tied to particular bits of land and dirt and air. I had just started to write the Easter sermon for York when my mother died. I had to set it down for a few days. I couldn't find a way to the resurrection part of this story so I went for a walk, not in Emmaus or Jerusalem or Galilee but along the river in West London where I live. And somewhere on that walk I remembered what it was or who it was I believed in; and that for all the particularity and 'back then-ness' of his story, he can still meet us today, on whatever road it is we are on.

Author's note

In these pages, we follow Jesus from his arrival in Jerusalem to his execution, remaining contemporary to the moment as reported, trying to imagine the events unfolding as though for the first time, in real time, without relying on any after-the-event wisdom that we might carry. I want to help us imagine being a follower, not always knowing what comes next, or how it ends, and without possessing the weight or comfort of the theological or cultural understanding that has gathered the far side of history – and the far side of his story.

The scripture references in this book come after the text rather than before, in order to help the reader 'walk' the week afresh, without it feeling too familiar, before then encouraging them to return to the Gospel accounts and hopefully find in them something new and encouraging, as well as something eternal and unchanging.

NOTES ON AN EXECUTION

1

Recognition: Palm Sunday

As we enter Holy Week and Jesus' last days, we sit on the far side of history and the other side of his story. We know what happens, and it is hard to unknow what we know, to unlearn two thousand years of culture and faith and theology. But the gospels at least allow us to imagine being there in the moment, as reported. To feel what it was to be one of His followers who, day by day, hour by hour, had no idea what was going to happen next. And today, we pick up the action in the village of Bethany, just a short ride from Jerusalem, where the disciples have come to celebrate the Passover . . .

*

If this crowd is anything to go by, it's going to be a great day and a great week. It is as though the good news has gone before them. Many of these people are here to celebrate the Passover that will end with the sacrifice of a lamb and a special meal; but they're clearly here for him.

3

His disciples are used to big crowds turning up out of curiosity, picking up on the rumours of healing and miracles and a new kind of teaching. If even a tenth of the rumours were true, he'd attract a crowd. But they did not expect this kind of reception, here in Jerusalem. There are days when they would quite like to keep him for themselves, rather than share him with everyone. But today is not one of those days. It looks as if the whole world is going after him.

They're a motley congregation. Made up of fishermen from Galilee, a lawyer, a tax collector. Women. Even children. Few here are rich or have great learning. Jesus has set the bar for following him low. To join this party, you just have to turn up and say yes.

Some of these people have already had their lives changed by him. There's a man from Jericho who had never seen a tree or the Temple until Jesus restored his sight. There is a woman he delivered from multiple afflictions, And, most incredibly, a man from just here in Bethany, whom Jesus raised from the dead.

This kind of power attracts attention.

When the people start to sing hosannas – to him! – it sounds as if each accolade is trying to outdo the last in acclaim: Son of David. Son of Man. King of Israel. The King of the World! Even though the disciples were themselves the first to believe all these titles – and more – they're taken aback.

Jesus doesn't look surprised. He looks as though he anticipated this. He rarely boasts about who he might be – and has gone out of his way to discourage it – but today, he is doing little to suppress the praise. He seems delighted by it and is enjoying his moment and receiving the praise as one worthy of it. He wears these weighty titles lightly, as though they were cut to fit him.

His followers truly believe this recognition is deserved. It is vindication for him and – by extension – for them. They've given up livelihoods and sacrificed a great deal to follow him thus far. They have thrown their all in with him. These endorsements confirm that they've made the right decision. And it's days like this that make following him feel like the best decision they've ever made.

This is a moment. They hope someone is keeping an account of it and writing it all down. Future musicians will surely compose songs in remembrance of this. With this kind of momentum, they could take the city today and maybe establish his kingdom by the end of the week.

When they reach the Mount of Olives and take in the view, even the prophet-killing city looks ready to welcome him. The sun is bathing Jerusalem in its golden light and Jerusalem obliges by reflecting back some of the glory. Perhaps this time it will recognise a *true* prophet when it sees one.

There is some concern among them that his popularity will cause him difficulties with the authorities. From a distance this crowd might be perceived as a protest movement, here to subvert the system in some way. It has been a year of simmering discontent and crushed rebellions; rebels challenging the status quo and claiming to be able to deliver Israel from oppression. The relationship between the occupier and the occupied is finely balanced. It wouldn't take much to tip it over.

But up close, this ragtag army and their Donkey King look incapable of threatening an empire. They sing hymns instead of making war cries, and wave serrated palms for flags. How could this Rabbi for Peace and his followers be a threat to anyone? If he were a *king* carrying a sword and riding a stallion at the head of an army, they might intervene. But no territory is being taken and no blood is being spilled. This is a low-security threat and the bemused expressions of the occupying soldiers confirm it: 'Carry on, enjoy your King for the Day, and your illusion of triumph, fools.' If there is subversion in this parade, the soldiers don't see it.

But this procession isn't an innocent, seemingly spontaneous happening. Jesus is making a bold statement, riding into Jerusalem on the back of Zechariah's prophecy: 'Shout aloud, O daughter Jerusalem! See, your king comes to you; triumphant and victorious is he, humble and riding on a donkey, on a colt, the foal of a donkey.' He's planned this. There are no accidents with him. From the moment they arrived in Bethany and arranged for the colt to be brought to him, he knew what he was doing. His every action as choreographed as the legions parading near Pilate's palace.

See how he rides over palms and cloaks and into the pages of prophecy without turning left or right to avoid the implications. He's done it before and they are sure he will do it again. Prophecies long planted in scripture burst to new life like spring whenever he passes.

The ones most likely to disapprove of this spectacle – the chief priests, elders and scribes – are not yet to be seen.

Perhaps when they reach the Temple they'll come forward and challenge him with the expected questions: 'Who do you think you are? The saviour of the world that Zechariah wrote about?' His followers are looking forward to that moment. They welcome the chance for the religious leaders to see for themselves who *their* Jesus really is.

But, just when the procession enters the Sheep's Gate, where the lambs are taken to the Temple for slaughter, Jesus stops and dismounts. And they wonder what he is going to do next. They are ready to ride this euphoria all the way to the Holy of Holies, but he just looks up at the Temple as if taking its full measure and then he turns and leaves.

'The time is not now,' he says. 'But we will come back here tomorrow.'

Gospel reading

Jesus' triumphal entry into Jerusalem

When they were approaching Jerusalem, at Bethphage and Bethany, near the Mount of Olives, he sent two of his disciples and said to them, 'Go into the village ahead of you, and immediately as you enter it you will find tied there a colt that has never been ridden; untie it and bring it. If anyone says to you, "Why are you doing this?" just say this: "The Lord needs it and will send it back here immediately." ' They went away and found a colt tied near a door, outside in the street. As they were untying it, some of the bystanders said to them, 'What are you doing, untying the colt?' They told them what Jesus had said, and they allowed them to take it. Then they brought the colt to Jesus and threw their cloaks on it, and he sat on it. Many people spread their cloaks on the road, and others spread leafy branches that they had cut in the fields. Then those who went ahead and those who followed were shouting,

'Hosanna!
Blessed is the one who comes in
the name of the Lord!
Blessed is the coming kingdom of
our ancestor David!
Hosanna in the highest heaven!'

Then he entered Jerusalem and went into the temple, and when he had looked around at everything, as it was already late, he went out to Bethany with the twelve.
(Mark 11:1–11)

Questions

- Imagine you were in this scene; are you more likely to be a willing participant or a careful observer?
- Until this moment Jesus has gone out of his way to play down his true identity; why do you think he does nothing to stop the crowd from praising him?
- How do you feel about physically demonstrative worship?

2

Confrontation: Monday

It is easy to forget and good to remember that the people following Jesus during his last days did so without knowing what was going to happen next. They were in the midst of a fast-moving story unfolding in real time and with little space to think things through. Every hour with Jesus brought something new, something unexpected. And today we pick up the action the day after the triumphal entry into Jerusalem. The disciples rise with the sun and prepare to follow Jesus to the Temple hoping to witness more great things from him.

*

They wake in Bethany still high on the sounds of praise that filled the air when they followed him into Jerusalem. Yesterday was a day that felt like a new holy day. And maybe in future they will have one to remember it by. Worship like that has rarely been seen outside the Temple. Perhaps this was what Jesus meant when he said to that woman in

Samaria, 'The hour is coming when you will worship the Father neither on this mountain nor in Jerusalem.'

But Jesus is not resting on yesterday's laurels. He is up early and sets out with his usual sense of purpose. He doesn't even have breakfast. Behind him, the sun is up over the wilderness where, just three years ago, he turned down Satan's offer of power-sharing, protection and land.

As Jesus walks ahead, the disciples compare notes. They agree: yesterday was a good day; no, it was a great day. The whole world was with him. His kingdom of justice and mercy campaign carried all. Everyone was a believer – for a day. There were no challenging parables, no confrontations. Just a lot of praising God and Jesus, and sometimes the two of them in the same breath.

Not everyone was glad. Perhaps it is never easy to watch people at worship when you are not worshipping yourself. To some the joy of the crowd appeared like madness, and their praise sounded like blasphemy. When Jesus was challenged by some priests to stop the people 'worshipping' him, his reply – that the very stones would cry out if he did – seemed to appal them. Will his words rebound off Jerusalem's walls and strike him back?

Before descending into the Kidron valley, Jesus stops to take in the view. The Temple dominates the city. The Temple *is* Jerusalem. Central to its life, and to its identity. It certainly has the dimensions to house a God. When you look at it from the valley, it's big enough to blot out the sun.

Herod built it to impress, and he particularly wanted to impress the Romans. And the Romans admire it. They can relate to its imperiousness, its muscular architecture, if not what takes place inside. The building was built to last a thousand years – maybe for ever. The stones can't be broken or breached. What God wouldn't be happy to live in a house like this?

But Jesus isn't happy. His face is set sternly against it. There's a fig tree in front of him that is framed by the Temple and he suddenly curses it for not bearing fruit. It seems harsh. It's not even the time for figs to bear fruit.

But he says to it, sharply, '**May no one ever eat fruit from you again.**'

As they go on, the disciples discuss his outburst. They are baffled by it. Perhaps he is hungry. They haven't had breakfast after all. But was he really equating the fruitless fig tree with the Temple? For that is where his gaze was fixed. If so, then it is some curse. They hope it is just one of his mysterious metaphors that will become clear later.

When they enter the Sheep's Gate, he turns left towards the Temple and enters the court of the Gentiles, where the impure and the foreign are allowed to worship. Something about this scene is riling him. He looks at it with such disdain it is hard to suppress the feeling that he is going to 'do' something.

And of course, he does something. When does he not? Even when he is perfectly still, he is doing something. He walks towards a money changer's table like someone calculating the force needed to turn it upside down and then he does just that! And while they are all taking this in, he brandishes a whip and effectively blocks the exits and entrances, and in a few beats manages to bring the well-oiled wheels of the Temple to a grinding halt. Then they hear him say, 'My **house shall be called a house of prayer for all the nations. But you have made it a den of robbers!'**

In a few moments, he trades in all the goodwill he gained yesterday and exchanges it to make this point. And if then he was straddling prophecy on Zechariah's donkey, today he quotes Jeremiah, the prophet who went out of his way to make himself unpopular in this city, and who was put in a pit for criticising Israel's treatment of the outsider. If you want to provoke religious power here, quote Jeremiah at it.

They see it now: his rant about the fruitless fig tree wasn't a random burst of irritability. It was a prelude to this. He *was* talking about the Temple. It has always been a contentious space, one part limestone, one part compromise. But it's not the style or construction of the building that seems to bother him; it's the apparent corruption permitted in its daily functioning. He sees a credibility gap between the practice and the fruit. There is little justice and mercy being shown here to those regarded as outsiders. And they worry: how far is he prepared to go in his championing of the impure and unworthy?

Not many of the startled sellers and pilgrims are able to comprehend his actions. But his actions are not for those who are permitted to make a living changing money. His words are for the ones who sanction it and who, so far, have been watching from a distance. The men in fine robes who are here, somewhere in the Temple space, watching from alcoves and hiding behind curtains.

Oh, Lord, it was all going so well until you did this! These people have followed you here, to hear you teach and maybe receive healing. We thought this was a non-violent protest. But this is crossing a line. This is going to attract attention and not in a good way. Do you want to get yourself killed? Because you're going the right way about it. A few of them think perhaps they should step forward and save him from himself.

When the chief priests, elders and scribes do appear, they are understandably affronted. This is their turf. They have a delicate operation to maintain here. The Romans are just waiting for the next excuse to shut things down and this man with his whip and table-flipping tantrum is providing the very excuse they might be looking for.

What happens in this space causes tremors throughout the land – and beyond. This status quo is hard won and requires complex compromises and a degree of collusion. It's not perfect. They are under occupation after all, but at least the occupation permits their people religious freedoms. And this man threatens to destroy this.

It is noticeable how the authorities don't ask *why* he is doing what he's doing. They almost don't want to know his reasons. Instead they ask him for some kind of sign that proves he has the right. A sign that underwrites his authority to behave this way.

How will he answer this? His followers would love him to demonstrate a little of that Lazarus-raising power, that Galilean lake-calming power. Just settle this argument once and for all. He might even win these men over to his message and then all would be well. But, they should know by now, that is not his way: **'Destroy this Temple, and in three days I will raise it up.'**

Does he have a death wish, a self-destructive urge? This statement is more baffling than the fig tree, and more outrageously offensive when they try to picture it. Even here, in a land well attuned to hyperbole, it is an exaggeration on another scale. He even talks about the Temple as though he owns the place!

This answer has the religious men shaking with barely suppressed rage. But it also sets his disciples' nerves on edge. Their Jesus is not bringing that sea-calming power to still the waters. After the smooth ride of yesterday, this road is roughing up. He has not come in peaceful protest. He has come as an earthquake, and the first tremors are starting to shake the foundations.

Gospel readings

Jesus curses the fig tree

On the following day, when they came from Bethany, he was hungry. Seeing in the distance a fig tree in leaf, he went to see whether perhaps he would find anything on it. When he came to it, he found nothing but leaves, for it was not the season for figs. He said to it, 'May no one ever eat fruit from you again.' And his disciples heard it.
(Mark 11:12–14)

Jesus cleanses the temple

Then they came to Jerusalem. And he entered the temple and began to drive out those who were selling and those who were buying in the temple, and he overturned the tables of the money changers and the seats of those who sold doves, and he would not allow anyone to carry anything through the temple. He was teaching and saying, 'Is it not written,

"My house shall be called a house of prayer for all the nations"?
But you have made it a den of robbers.'

And when the chief priests and the scribes heard it, they kept looking for a way to kill him, for they were afraid of him because the whole crowd was spellbound by his teaching. And when evening came, Jesus and his disciples went out of the city.
(Mark 11:15–19)

Questions

- Why do you think Jesus curses the fig tree?
- What do you think Jesus is really upset by when he turns over the tables of the money changers?
- Are there things that Jesus said or did that you have found difficult?

3
Interrogation: Tuesday

We all stand this side of his story. We have had time to try and make sense of what took place in the last, furious days of Jesus' life. But imagine being there, following him from one extraordinary incident to another, barely having a second to draw breath. Today is another breathless day, as we follow him back to the Temple where he is about to astonish his followers, the crowd, as well as the authorities, who can no longer afford to ignore him.

*

'Let's hope he gets back to being the Jesus they know,' is how they feel as they enter the Temple courts, ready to hear him teach. Back to being the Jesus who answers questions with questions. Or with stories that see through to the heart of the matter. That's how they like him: being the cleverest rabbi in the room. It makes them look good, too.

They can't predict what will occur – can they ever? – but some kind of controversy seems inevitable. That much they can prophesy! His radiant charisma is a two-edged sword, relentlessly cutting through to the truth – and the truth, his followers are learning, hurts.

They still love him and will follow him all the way; of that they have no doubt. He's still carrying the crowd, but yesterday was rough. His 'teaching' was too physical, too obviously confrontational. Much more of that and the chief priests, scribes and elders, who have largely kept away, will have to stamp their authority.

And today, the authorities are ready for him and they have the look of people about to take back the high ground. They have a question for him. One they've been dying to ask him: **'By what authority are you doing these things?'**

At first, they wonder what the chief priests mean by *'these things'*. Do they mean all the things Jesus has done since he began his ministry: the signs and wonders, the healings; raising a man from the dead? Or do they mean the events since he arrived at the Temple, being hailed a saviour and not denying it. Or his violent shutting down of the Temple yesterday?

They should really ask him about the signs and wonders. But they never do ask the obvious question, such as: 'Is it true that the blind see, or that the dead are raised?' Instead, they ask him the authority question because authority is their specialist subject.

His followers want to shout out: 'He gets his authority from his Father, the Lord God, because he is his Son!' But he doesn't say this. He knows it's a trap – a Son-of-Mantrap. Less about wanting to understand, more about catching him out and, with luck, getting him to testify against himself.

The question about authority is really a professional question. Teaching in the Temple is the responsibility of the religious elite and they have to manage and monitor the order of services. This is a huge operation and Passover week the biggest religious event of the year. Anyone interfering with this will have to explain themselves.

But he says, 'I will ask you one question; answer me, and I will tell you . . . Did the baptism of John come from heaven, or was it of human origin?'

Of course! He answers a question with a question. He just can't help himself! He doesn't do it to make himself look good – although it does! He does it to expose the truth. To bring the real issue to light.

And what is the real issue here? Well. Jesus asking them about John the Baptist cuts to the core of it. Religion is their job; John was a prophet – they must have an opinion. But their dealings with John at the time exposed a weakness in the establishment. John's arbitrary execution was caused by a ruler's overreaction and it was embarrassing for the religious elite; they knew the people believed that John was a prophet but they couldn't admit he was because of their collusion with Herod. And now, here comes Jesus, another embarrassment to the religious elite, and a possible threat to Rome, and someone the people say is a prophet – and maybe much more. Are they intending to do the same to him?

Jesus' followers hope that's where the parallel ends.

But his presence is galling to the chief priests. Not helped by this rabble of ill-educated acolytes, basking in their rabbi's reflected glory. For the crowd, this is good sport. The chief priests are squirming a little, as they calculate and search for both the least unpopular and most face-saving answer. An answer that avoids unpleasant consequences and causes the least damage to their status.

'We don't know,' they say. And Jesus keeps *his* word and leaves it there.

The Herodians come next – and from their faces they seem sure they have a killer question. They grease it with insincere flattery: 'You being one who teaches the ways of God to us.' Before asking him: 'Is it lawful to pay taxes to Caesar or not?'

They're sure they have him now. He can't answer this without perjuring himself. It's a slippery political question and another trap. And Jesus says as much: **'Why are you putting me to the test?'** His question is rhetorical, because he knows exactly why they are testing him in this way. As do the crowd.

Jesus asks to see the coin and then asks whose image it shows, confirming that it is Tiberius Caesar's. They think he's got one foot in the trap. But then Jesus delivers a line that resonates throughout the Temple and all the way to the Roman camp: **'Give to Caesar the things that are Caesar's and to God the things that are God's!'**

He is so brilliant!

And they're so glad he is theirs! If today the Temple is a theological coliseum, where men fight with weapons of wit and wisdom, then he is the champion. He's outnumbered and cornered but it is still no contest. Behold our man! Are we not entertained? The watching scribes should be writing down every single word that comes from his mouth, instead of trying to put their words into his!

All day, Jesus teaches hard and fast. But with such a light touch. There is so much to discuss as they head back to Bethany, exhausted but exhilarated. They can't decide which of his stellar interactions was his best. Or which caused the most consternation among the religious elite: was it the authority question, the tax question, or was it the story about the vineyard that he told just before they left the Temple?

His stories are like Trojan horses: smuggling armies of dangerous truths into the enemy camp, which later in the day burst out with devastating effect. And this one was devastating.

To see the faces of the priests when he'd finished telling it. They knew he'd spoken against them. The crowd knew it, too. And it was probably only the applause of the crowd that prevented them from acting against him right there in broad daylight.

Everyone got it. The vineyard is Israel and it is being poorly managed, neglected, ill tended. Only a fool could walk the length and breadth of this land and conclude that it was a land of milk and honey, upholding justice and mercy. Those servants in the story were the prophets trying to bring Israel back to its better self and refer it back to the plumb line of God's revelation. To point out that its essential values have been lost. That it is meant to be a 'light to the nations', to feed the poor and look after the alien in the land.

It always falls to the prophets to say the difficult thing to the powerful! But if you truly love God you have to hate the evil things done in his name and call them out. Even if it kills you. As to the identity of the son in his story, well, they know it's him; but the disciples would rather it wasn't literally him. Perhaps it can just be a salutary tale rather than a prophecy that becomes history.

Today, Jesus has won the arguments, and even more followers, but he is racking up the offences: Son of God Claimant, Temple Threatener, Heart Motive Challenger, Defier of Oppressive Power. His popularity continues to protect him, but for how long?

It feels that with every urgent and challenging truth he delivers, he takes another step towards serious trouble. It's nearly Wednesday. At the rate he's going, he may not make it the other side Passover.

Gospel readings

Jesus' authority is questioned

Again they came to Jerusalem. As he was walking in the temple, the chief priests, the scribes, and the elders came to him and said, 'By what authority are you doing these things? Who gave you this authority to do them?' Jesus said to them, 'I will ask you one question; answer me, and I will tell you by what authority I do these things. Did the baptism of John come from heaven, or was it of human origin? Answer me.' They argued with one another, 'What should we say? If we say, "From heaven," he will say, "Why then did you not believe him?" But shall we say, "Of human origin"?'— they were afraid of the crowd, for all regarded John as truly a prophet. So they answered Jesus, 'We do not know.' And Jesus said to them, 'Neither will I tell you by what authority I am doing these things.'
(Mark 11:27–33)

The parable of the wicked tenants

Then he began to speak to them in parables. 'A man planted a vineyard, put a fence around it, dug a pit for the winepress, and built a watchtower; then he leased it to tenants and went away. When the season came, he sent a slave to the tenants to collect from them his share of the produce of the vineyard. But they seized him and beat him and sent him away empty-handed. And again he sent another slave to them; this one they beat over the head and insulted. Then he sent another, and that one they killed. And so it was with many others; some they beat, and others they killed. He had still one other, a beloved son. Finally he sent him to them, saying, "They will respect my son." But those tenants said to one another, "This is the heir; come, let us kill him, and the inheritance will be ours." So they seized him, killed him, and threw him out of the vineyard. What then will the owner of the vineyard do? He will come and destroy the tenants and give the vineyard to others. Have you not read this scripture:

> "The stone that the builders rejected
>   has become the cornerstone;
> this was the Lord's doing,
>   and it is amazing in our eyes"?'

When they realized that he had told this parable against them, they wanted to arrest him, but they feared the crowd. So they left him and went away.
(Mark 12:1–12)

The question about paying taxes

Then they sent to him some Pharisees and some Herodians to trap him in what he said. And they came and said to him, 'Teacher, we know that you are sincere and show deference to no one, for you do not regard people with partiality but teach the way of God in accordance with truth. Is it lawful to pay taxes to Caesar or not? Should we pay them, or should we not?' But knowing their hypocrisy, he said to them, 'Why are you putting me to the test? Bring me a denarius and let me see it.' And they brought one. Then he said to them, 'Whose head is this and whose title?' They answered, 'Caesar's.' Jesus said to them, 'Give to Caesar the things that are Caesar's and to God the things that are God's.' And they were utterly amazed at him. (Mark 12:13–17)

Questions

- Why do you think Jesus speaks in parables?
- What do you think Jesus means by 'the things that are Caesar's' and 'the things that are God's'?
- Have you found yourself torn between the authority of Jesus and those of the world?

4

Anointing: Wednesday

We are in the middle of *our* Holy Week. For Jesus' followers it is two days before Passover. We know these are his last days, but his disciples are hoping this is just the beginning; that the world will soon know who their Jesus is. But there have been troubling signs. Jesus is not making this easy. As they approach Passover some question whether his way is the best way. Meanwhile, enemies without and within are starting to make their moves.

*

The childlike abandon with which they skipped into Jerusalem, and the sense that a decisive victory was imminent, has been replaced by anxiety. Following him has always had a bearable lightness; but the way is getting heavier with every step.

Jesus has been utterly himself, as he always is, but there is a quickening pace to his teaching. He moves like a man on a mission, like someone giving the best of themselves before leaving. He is emptying his treasury, throwing gold, gems and pearls, like so much seed, on the Temple floor. Even the dogs it seems are welcome to these crumbs.

There has been little time for them to ask, 'What do you think he meant by that?', or 'What just happened back there?' It is hard to see everything that's going on. He, of course, sees it all. While they are drawn to the showy moments, he sees the little things and makes something great from them. Like that widow in the Temple, putting everything she had into the treasury. They missed it – their eyes elsewhere – but he saw it and made her look like the most important person in God's house.

There is a growing animus towards Jesus. Today, he again made the religious elite look bad in front of a lot of people, and that will have hurt their pride. As the gatekeepers, they have legitimate concerns about the threat he poses, to their status but also to the status quo. With his every utterance, Jesus threatens this.

Doubts about where this is going are starting to tap the disciples on the shoulder. 'Where he goes, we go' has always been their psalm, and so far they have not looked back. But part of them longs for the Galilean days – his easy manifesto of light burdens, simple kingdom principles, protocols of love and acceptance. It was easy to follow this.

Maybe his message gets lost in the noise of the big city, with the sophisticates and the busy. Like that poor rich man today, who asked how he might enter his kingdom. The look on his face when Jesus told him what he needed to do. That broad highway of his seems to be narrowing.

On the way back to Bethany, things take a morbid turn. The subject of death – his death – comes up again. He will not let it lie. And although he's been trying to prepare them for this eventuality – even describing the manner of it – it just won't sink in. They don't want it to sink in. The idea leaves them cold.

They look once more over the city, and his words are valedictory, almost resigned. Where they see a city of peace, he sees a violent and corrupt monstrosity that devours prophets and spits out the truth. As they marvel at the Temple – so impressive, so permanent – he sees it in ruins. He then describes, in great detail, what is to come – and it is not good news.

His apocalypse has a certain thrill. As long as the dreadful outcomes he describes lie in some future, beyond *their* own lifespan. As long as future generations get to face all those wars and rumours of wars, earthquakes and environmental disasters; counterfeit Messiahs, neighbours killing neighbours. Nations seeking the total destruction of nations.

So, of course, their first question isn't, 'Does this have to happen?', but, 'When will this happen?' Instead of giving them a time and a date, he tells them an unnerving story, featuring his signature character – the Son of Man who, having to go on a long journey, leaves his house in the care of his servants. Before leaving, he asks them to watch for his return. He may come back in the evening or as the cock crows; they won't know the hour, they just have to watch. Of course, this Son of Man sounds like him. And the servants are surely them.

Why does he insist on talking about endings – his ending, Jerusalem's ending, the end of all things! – and why does he have to include them in his denouements?

They return to Bethany, to the house of Simon the leper. Jesus relishes Simon's company. No good Jew enters a leper's house, let alone eats with one, but Jesus doesn't see things the way they do. Sometimes, when they try to see things the way he does, they have to look away.

They're hoping that tonight they might finally get some time alone with him. But, while they're eating, an uninvited woman enters the room, carrying a long-necked alabaster jar. It is hard to know what is more shocking: a woman entering a room full of men eating or what she starts doing next.

She breaks the neck of the jar and pours what smells like spikenard ointment over Jesus' head. She runs her oily hands through his hair. The sweet, heady, expensive scent causes a stench of offence. It is an embarrassment. The only person who seems comfortable with it is him.

They ask her, 'What are you doing?' And Judas says what everyone is thinking: what a waste of money. That's 300 denarii right there. Money they could have given to the poor. Judas should know. He's the one holding the purse strings and knows the price of everything. A year's wages – for this act?

Jesus then says what 'this' act is.

'Leave her be. She knows what she's doing. It is an act of love. Of generosity. You will always have the poor, and find ways to be kind to them – but you won't always have me.'

34

This woman has had an insight into *their* Jesus and she has only just arrived. She knows who he is.

It gets worse: she starts to wash his feet – with her hair! – and shower him with unadulterated love. They almost can't watch. Does he have no sense of boundaries, that he allows her to touch him like this? How far is he prepared to go to include the impure? Too far for some of them.

He is always showing them what being a follower looks like: do not lord it over others, be like a child, the last shall be first. And here, in this place, he does it again. Only this time it takes an unknown stranger – and a woman at that – to flip their hierarchal thinking over, like those tables in the Temple. The table flipping was easier to accept than this!

And now she starts to weep over him. It's the kind of weeping that people do when they have lost someone they love. It's as though she's grieving him. They want her to stop, but he doesn't. As far as Jesus is concerned, she has completely understood the moment. She knows who he is and where he is going. She knows what *they* are refusing to accept: that he is going to die and quite soon. Her act is a prophetic act, and she is anointing him for burial, with spice worthy of a king. Surely when Jesus is prepared for burial, it will be by a high priest in the Temple, not by a woman in the house of a leper.

This intervention forces them to think again about the way this story is going. This mission was simpler when they were challenging imperial and religious power and the collusions required to maintain it. But his permissive acceptance of the unclean is more difficult to follow. His intimacy with impurity keeps exposing their impurity.

This mission is about more than transforming the powers out there. It is about the powers that lie within – the lust, the envy, the pride – within the heart. And they wonder: can they really play a part in such a mission, when their own hearts betray them, hour by hour?

Gospel readings

The widow's offering

He sat down opposite the treasury and watched the crowd putting money into the treasury. Many rich people put in large sums. A poor widow came and put in two small copper coins, which are worth a penny. Then he called his disciples and said to them, 'Truly I tell you, this poor widow has put in more than all those who are contributing to the treasury. For all of them have contributed out of their abundance, but she out of her poverty has put in everything she had, all she had to live on.'
(Mark 12:41–4)

The destruction of the temple foretold

As he came out of the temple, one of his disciples said to him, 'Look, Teacher, what large stones and what large buildings!' Then Jesus asked him, 'Do you see these great buildings? Not one stone will be left here upon another; all will be thrown down.' When he was sitting on the Mount of Olives opposite the temple, Peter, James, John, and Andrew asked him privately, 'Tell us, when will this be, and what will be the sign that all these things are about to be accomplished?' Then Jesus began to say to them, 'Beware that no one leads you astray. Many will come in my name and say, "I am he!" and they will lead many astray. When you hear of wars and rumours of wars, do not be alarmed; this must take place, but the end is still to come. For nation will rise against nation and kingdom against kingdom; there will be earthquakes in various

places; there will be famines. This is but the beginning of the birth pangs.'
(Mark 13:1–8)

The desolating sacrilege

'But when you see the desolating sacrilege set up where it ought not to be (let the reader understand), then those in Judea must flee to the mountains; the one on the housetop must not go down or enter to take anything from the house; the one in the field must not turn back to get a coat. Woe to those who are pregnant and to those who are nursing infants in those days! Pray that it may not be in winter. For in those days there will be suffering, such as has not been from the beginning of the creation that God created until now and never will be. And if the Lord had not cut short those days, no one would be saved, but for the sake of the elect, whom he chose, he has cut short those days. And if anyone says to you at that time, "Look! Here is the Messiah!" or "Look! There he is!" – do not believe it. False messiahs and false prophets will appear and produce signs and wonders, to lead astray, if possible, the elect. But be alert; I have already told you everything.'
(Mark 13:14–23)

The coming of the Son of Man

'But in those days, after that suffering,

the sun will be darkened,
    and the moon will not give its light,

and the stars will be falling from heaven,
and the powers in the heavens will be shaken.

'Then they will see "the Son of Man coming in clouds" with great power and glory. Then he will send out the angels and gather the elect from the four winds, from the ends of the earth to the ends of heaven.'
(Mark 13:24–7)

The anointing at Bethany

While he was at Bethany in the house of Simon the leper, as he sat at the table, a woman came with an alabaster jar of very costly ointment of nard, and she broke open the jar and poured the ointment on his head. But some were there who said to one another in anger, 'Why was the ointment wasted in this way? For this ointment could have been sold for more than three hundred denarii and the money given to the poor.' And they scolded her. But Jesus said, 'Let her alone; why do you trouble her? She has performed a good service for me. For you always have the poor with you, and you can show kindness to them whenever you wish, but you will not always have me. She has done what she could; she has anointed my body beforehand for its burial. Truly I tell you, wherever the good news is proclaimed in the whole world, what she has done will be told in remembrance of her.'
(Mark 14:3–9)

Questions

- Can you think of examples where you have given beyond what is comfortable. How did it feel afterwards?
- How do you feel about Jesus' apocalyptic descriptions; do they have anything to say to us now?
- Jesus always seems to notice people at the margins; how do we do the same?

5
Parting: Maundy Thursday

We come to this story knowing what happens next. But the ones following Jesus, in the last days of his life, had no idea. For them, the events we remember as the Last Supper, the washing of the disciples' feet, the betrayal, have not yet happened. Or been written down in scripture. For them there is no Easter. There is no Eucharist. There are no churches. No one has memorialised these events in stone or song, egg tempura or gold leaf. The calendar has not yet been set to 'Before him' and 'After him'. Crucially (and even this word doesn't yet have full meaning!) there has been no crucifixion. On this day, Jesus is still with them. And we join them now, in the upper room of a house in Jerusalem, where they have gathered to celebrate Passover.

*

They're together at last. In the room he arranged for them to enjoy this Passover meal. Getting here wasn't straightforward. Jerusalem's lanes were choked with pilgrims trying to get to their own celebrations. And his instructions were particular: find a man carrying a pitcher of water. He will lead you to a house where there will be a room for us to eat together. The prearrangement was like that moment in Bethany – was it really just five days ago? – when he asked them to find the donkey's colt for him to ride into Jerusalem, in triumph.

They wonder: how does he have time to plan ahead? He is so in the moment of every situation – so fully present. But there are no accidents with him. He always has a plan. Detail and timing. Care and preparation. He *is* always the good shepherd, steering them to where they need to be. And they're grateful for it. It's easy to get lost in Jerusalem. And it is easy to lose sight of him.

But he's here now. And finally they have him to themselves. The needy crowds, the needling religious leaders, are busy with their own Passovers.

It is true, their love for him has made them possessive. He has so many people demanding things of him. All week they have shared him with the general public, the religious authorities. Everyone wants a piece of him. And he seems to have an endless supply of himself. This immense capacity and patience. Giving himself is like breathing to him – it is his very lifeblood.

They have so much to discuss. The things they've witnessed these last few days could fill books. All week he has been questioned by others, now it is their turn to ask some questions. Such as: will the end of all things that he prophesied occur in their lifetime? Or can he tell them again how he intends to rebuild the Temple in three days?

And when that woman anointed him with expensive oil last night, did he really believe she was preparing him for burial?

As they settle down to eat, Jesus is pensive. It is no wonder. Think of the things he has going on in that mind of his. He sees so much – in the now and in the not-yet. He can meet someone for the first time and know more about them than they know of themselves. Like that woman at the well, or the man at the pools of Bethesda. Or them! He can feel someone touch the hem of his garment when in a crowd, and perceive his own death in a woman pouring oil over him.

He starts by telling them how much he has desired to be with them in this moment. And it makes them feel – if it were possible – even more loved. He also makes them feel needed. Could it be that he actually *does* need them? That he can't do this without them? It's always a surprise when he is vulnerable with them, but it makes them feel closer to him.

The Passover meal begins with a prayer. They remember their people's deliverance from oppressive power. And the God who saved them. Some picture the Red Sea parting, others the lamb's blood on the doors. The familiar ritual steadies their nerves and restores them to a simple unity of purpose.

But then, just as he gives them the bread and the wine, he changes the words. They are so going through the motions of the familiar ritual, they almost miss it. He actually says the bread of affliction is *his* body, and the cup of redemption is *his* blood. And then he extends his arms to pray and invites all people, beyond even their own kin, to join him in a new kind of Passover!

They've been with him long enough to get used to changing the way they do things; but this one is not easy. The inauguration of a new Passover? The bread and the wine his body and his blood? And now, he is inviting them to remember him with this meal – as often as they meet. But how do they remember a person who is still very much alive and present? Will he in fact be dead when they next meet – and when will that be? And what will they remember when they meet? This meal itself? Or the new meaning that he has invested in it?

This is more than a parting from what they have always known. It is a profound and difficult new reality. And it is frightening in its implications. For, if he is making himself a kind of Passover lamb, does that mean he must die? And if they partake in him, do they have to share in his destiny?

His story arc keeps bending towards death. His death. And he is telling them again that until they accept this, they can't be a part of his story. If they are to partake in his story, they have to partake in him. His death is the blood-theme that runs through this narrative, and he will not let it go until they get it, until it has bled into their own understanding. Even though he distils this instruction into an essence they can taste and actually swallow. It is hard to swallow.

In the last few days, following him has lost some of that bearable lightness. Their tread has been getting heavier. They still see themselves as part of a mission that will accomplish something tangible. They imagine extending the kingdom, spreading the good news. But how does this fit into that narrative? What they think needs to be accomplished and what he thinks must be accomplished are not the same thing.

They are just a few mouthfuls into the meal when he utters the words, **'One of you will betray me.'**

Most of them have the same first thought: *'Well, I know it's not me'*; and then the same question: *'But who could it be?'* Did they hear him right? Or has he misheard something or misunderstood something? Then again, when has he ever been wrong?

Jesus is not asking them to guess. He identifies his betrayer as Judas, by dipping his bread into the wine – the wine that they have just been asked to see as his blood. Judas does not really protest his innocence. Just as they are thinking, 'Judas, how could you?' they are also asking, 'How could you *what*?' What has he done? How has he betrayed him, and to whom? And when did he get the time to do this? Judas has been with them every day. He's part of this story.

When they sing the song of deliverance, at the end of the meal, their voices crack with fragmenting emotion. This revelation threatens their group, possibly their whole mission. Just when Jesus shows them what true integration looks like, along comes this threat of disintegration.

But they are not thinking straight; they are not even addressing the implications of what this betrayal means. And they have already forgotten the things Jesus was saying about his death. Instead, they start a nervy, defensive jostling for positions of power, in whatever kingdom is to come. They want to know who is going to run the show if Jesus is no longer with them.

By way of answer, he causes another embarrassing situation. Just as he did last night at the house of Simon the leper, with that unnamed woman. He stands, takes off his outer garment, finds a towel, pours water into a basin and starts to wash their feet. Their filthy, calloused feet that have followed him all the way from Galilee via Jericho to Jerusalem. It is so awkward, not least because he's washing *their* feet, and that is something only a servant does. Which of course is the point he is making. There are no empty gestures with him.

He insists on washing the feet of everyone present. When they object – as Peter does most adamantly – he again asks: do you want to be a part of me? Because this is what you must do.

As he washes them, they feel the gentlest reprimand in his fingers. A resetting of their thinking. He's been showing them all week, and every day for the last three years: children before adults; donkeys for stallions; masters as servants; dying in order to live. Their topsy-turvy king keeps turning things upside down, because the world has things the wrong way round. They know this is the way of the world, they just keep forgetting. And he knows this about them, so he keeps reminding them. What will happen when he's not here to remind them?

They know too that everything he does points to what the Father is like. But this action describes a God that does not fit their ideas of what God should be. A self-sacrificing foot-washing God who gets down on his knees, and washes them, is too much to comprehend. This unfamiliar God is too familiar. This visceral, surgical love cuts too deep.

On this night, when they remember their God parting the sea, they sense a parting of other things, of ideas and traditions, and perhaps a parting of their ways. In this very moment of togetherness, he has introduced a note of departure. He tells them this parting is necessary. He tells them that he must go to come back. He must die to live. Be raised to rise. But they still want the story to go their way, not his.

They leave the room and head back towards the Mount of Olives, via Gethsemane. As they go they no longer feel in step with him. And they wonder: *does* he need them? Can they be of any help to him now? It feels as though he needs to do something only he can accomplish on his own.

At the place where the oil is pressed, the whole night is pressing down on them. And then Jesus confirms their worst fears. He tells them that their ways *will* part. And that even before the sun rises, they are all going to leave him. Alone.

Gospel readings

The Passover with the disciples

On the first day of Unleavened Bread, when the Passover lamb is sacrificed, his disciples said to him, 'Where do you want us to go and make the preparations for you to eat the Passover?' So he sent two of his disciples, saying to them, 'Go into the city, and a man carrying a jar of water will meet you; follow him, and wherever he enters, say to the owner of the house, "The Teacher asks: Where is my guest room where I may eat the Passover with my disciples?" He will show you a large room upstairs, furnished and ready. Make preparations for us there.' So the disciples set out and went to the city and found everything as he had told them, and they prepared the Passover meal.

When it was evening, he came with the twelve. And when they had taken their places and were eating, Jesus said, 'Truly I tell you, one of you will betray me, one who is eating with me.' They began to be distressed and to say to him one after another, 'Surely, not I?' He said to them, 'It is one of the twelve, one who is dipping bread into the bowl with me. For the Son of Man goes as it is written of him, but woe to that one by whom the Son of Man is betrayed! It would have been better for that one not to have been born.' (Mark 14:12–21)

The institution of the Lord's Supper

While they were eating, he took a loaf of bread, and after blessing it he broke it, gave it to them, and said, 'Take; this is my body.' Then he took a cup, and after giving thanks he

gave it to them, and all of them drank from it. He said to them, 'This is my blood of the covenant, which is poured out for many. Truly I tell you, I will never again drink of the fruit of the vine until that day when I drink it new in the kingdom of God.'
(Mark 14:22–25)

Peter's denial foretold

When they had sung the hymn, they went out to the Mount of Olives. And Jesus said to them, 'You will all fall away, for it is written,

"I will strike the shepherd,
and the sheep will be scattered."

'But after I am raised up, I will go before you to Galilee.' Peter said to him, 'Even though all fall away, I will not.' Jesus said to him, 'Truly I tell you, this day, this very night, before the cock crows twice, you will deny me three times.' But he said vehemently, 'Even though I must die with you, I will not deny you.' And all of them said the same.
(Mark 14:26–31)

Jesus prays in Gethsemane

They went to a place called Gethsemane, and he said to his disciples, 'Sit here while I pray.' He took with him Peter and James and John and began to be distressed and agitated. And he said to them, 'My soul is deeply grieved, even to death; remain here, and keep awake.' And going a little farther, he threw himself on the ground and prayed that, if it were possible, the hour might pass from him. He said, 'Abba, Father, for you all things are possible; remove this cup from me, yet not what I want but what you want.' He came and found them sleeping, and he said to Peter, 'Simon, are you asleep? Could you not keep awake one hour? Keep awake and pray that you may not come into the time of trial; the spirit indeed is willing, but the flesh is weak.' And again he went away and prayed, saying the same words. And once more he came and found them sleeping, for their eyes were very heavy, and they did not know what to say to him. He came a third time and said to them, 'Are you still sleeping and taking your rest? Enough! The hour has come; the Son of Man is betrayed into the hands of sinners. Get up, let us be going. Look, my betrayer is at hand.'

(Mark 14:32–42)

The betrayal and arrest of Jesus

Immediately, while he was still speaking, Judas, one of the twelve, arrived, and with him there was a crowd with swords and clubs, from the chief priests, the scribes, and the elders. Now the betrayer had given them a sign, saying, 'The one I will kiss is the man; arrest him and lead him away under guard.' So when he came, he went up to him at once and said, 'Rabbi!' and kissed him. Then they laid hands on him and arrested him. But one of those who stood near drew his sword and struck the slave of the high priest, cutting off his ear. Then Jesus said to them, 'Have you come out with swords and clubs to arrest me as though I were a rebel? Day after day I was with you in the temple

teaching, and you did not arrest me. But let the scriptures be fulfilled.' All of them deserted him and fled.
(Mark 14:43–50)

Questions

- What does it mean to you to break bread and drink wine?
- Has your understanding of this changed and in what ways?
- Have you ever felt abandoned by God; and have you ever felt that there are times when you have abandoned him?

6
Noise: Good Friday – first meditation

Bad news comes in the night, by torchlight and with a
kiss.
And there is no time to collect our things – or even our
thoughts.

The sun rises over an indifferent city.
We wake to the noise of pride having its way.

At the house of the high priest, men have gathered
to confirm a verdict already decided.

And we watch – unseen, from a distance – and unable to
intervene.
Trying to deny our impotence.

Yesterday you were in our grasp,
but today you are in *their* clutches.

Noise

We hear the growl of worldly power clearing its throat
and raising its voice in condemnation.

The unjust dispensing injustice to the just
makes a particular sound:

At first, it strains, not quite believing itself
(especially when confronted with one who does).

Then it raises its voice, it eggs itself on.
And in no time, it sounds like righteousness.

The assembled want to get this over and done with.
Before you throw another kingdom seed on their land.

They have seen the quick-forming fruit
you leave in your wake:

The walking lame, the seeing blind,
the born-again dead.

The things that make the people glad
have made the powerful envy.

You have become popular.
The sooner they shut you up, the better.

They have seen a narrow opening.
And they are going to force you through it.

Good Friday – first meditation

You are guilty of a litany of crimes:

You've kissed decaying lepers. Spoken to the unacceptable
and the despicable. Eaten with the awful.

You have said too much. You have not been restrained.
You exaggerated. You Temple-destroying, table-flipper.
You insulted the wrong people.

You are guilty of claiming that most vital of territories:
the human heart.

You reduced a well-established set of laws to two
with one imperative:
to Love. (How dare you?)

You are guilty of being adored.
Only God should be adored. Are you a God?

Your silence is infuriating – it makes them sound loud.
And look bad. But who is looking bad now?

The tables are turned and the Temple is still standing.
Solid and squat, and eternal.

You have given them a lot of rope.
All the wood and nails they need.

They just need your word.
That you are who *they* say you're not.

Noise

Here are some names.
Do you recognise any or all of these?

We think: Don't say it, Jesus! Don't give them what they
want!
Keep silent – the way you are now. The way we are now!

There is merit in denying things.
Especially if it saves your skin.

But no. You can't not speak the truth
even if it kills you!

'I am.'

*

Perhaps the Romans will work out you're no threat.
Although Pilate's got a lot on his mind, his hands are tied.

He's a reputation and palace to maintain.
He'll do anything for a quiet life.

You could give him the truth.
But then would he recognise the truth if it was staring
back at him?

From back here, among a crowd whose blood is up,
we can't hear what you're saying.

Good Friday – first meditation

No doubt you are speaking truth,
but will this power hear what you're saying in all this
noise?

Now there is a symphony of self-preservation going on
between the powers that be.

Status and the status quo
are bound in intimate collusion.

They want the murderer released and the peacemaker
murdered.
They want to cause you harm and they want to cause us
grief.

Give the people what *we* want – and let what we want be
what they want.
It is for the good of us all that this one man dies.

This mob is loud.
Should we make some noise for you?

Do we charge forward and seize you?
Are we meant to intervene?
But how could we? We are not strong. We are not even
together.

We believe in you.
But are we brave enough to stand up for what we believe
in in the face of such violence?

Noise

Last week the whole world wanted a piece of you;
now they all want to tear you to pieces.

We remain at a distance.
Close enough to witness, but not enough to interfere.

Is this God's will?
Is this what you meant at Passover: that you are the lamb?

A hundred thousand lambs have been slaughtered
today.
Enough blood to make a Red Sea.
But who is going to part it now?

What intervention can we expect at this eleventh hour?

Oh Jesus. Stop being so stubborn, so committed and
faithful.
Stop with your selflessness – just this once – for our
sakes.

We still have things to do. Life to live. Kingdom to come.
Good news to spread. Stories to tell. Things to achieve.

We've sacrificed a lot for you.
Given up livelihoods and homes and friends.

But no: you keep your peace.
And the Romans keep the peace of Rome.

Good Friday – first meditation

Vengeance has its own special motion.
The wheels within wheels are turning.

You are taken away to be taken apart,
and this body of ours is being broken up.

You have been their scourge and now they are scourging
you.
You aren't going to save your skin.
And they are not saving your skin.

They whip and strip you and humiliate you.
The world can't handle you. So, it will manhandle you.

Will you quote Jeremiah at them?
Or are you walking towards another prophecy?
God, let it not be that one:

'He was oppressed and afflicted, but he did not open his
mouth.'
It sounds remarkably like you.

Around you the noise of the world.
But you – silent.

Please do something! You've slipped away from trouble
before
– when the time wasn't yet.

Noise

You said you'd love us with a mother's care.
But will you now leave us to face death? Alone?

They are mocking you for the things you said:
King of the Jews, Temple Destroyer, Son of God.

In this mood, the noise of the world pierces.
It leaves our ears ringing.

If there are other voices, we can't hear them.
The brute power of people's desires can't be silenced.

The ones in control have lost control.
They are stripping you naked.
And there is no stopping naked power.

This is not the way. There was another way. But we have
lost our way.

7
Silence:
Good Friday –
second meditation

You rode into Jerusalem a king on a song of
prophecy.
Now you stumble away, with a terrible crown.

The palms and robes have been cleared from the
streets.
They are piled on the rubbish heap at Golgotha.

We want to follow you.
But not the way you're going now, not there.

You asked us to remember you, but not like this:
carrying your cross, bent double, bleeding, naked.

We hardly recognise you. We did not say yes to this.
We said yes to the water-walking, food-multiplying,
dead-raiser.

Silence

But not the crushed man full of sorrows,
heading to an arbitrary and unjust execution.

We had a good story to tell – until now.
But no one will want to tell this story, if this is how it
ends.

Evil wins. Power crushes. The sick remain sick. The
dead stay dead.
Children are silenced, the leaders lord it. And you die.

Your mission was meant to lead to a victory,
to some sort of crowning triumph, not to Golgotha.

The world is having its day.
It would rather let a good man die and a murderer live.

Not that it's given you much thought.
We hear the silence of the world.
Look, how they carry on with their business, with their
lives.

The day has enough trouble of its own without having
to watch this.
Another execution of someone who probably deserves
it.

And even if you're innocent, so what?
Innocent people die every day. What's so special about
you?

Good Friday – second meditation

We may not feel your pain, but we share in your
humiliation.
Only yesterday, we were so sure of ourselves – and you.

Oh, Jesus: they're going to win. The victory is going to
be theirs.
Their way *is* the way! Not your way.

The powerful, the loudmouths, the clever,
the pious, the sorted and satisfied.

The colluders, the oppressors, the occupiers, the mob,
the torturers,
the mockers, the indifferent are going to have the final
word.

Look at you. Dressed up like the topsy-turvy king,
newly and cruelly crowned.

We can't look.
It would be better for us to put out our eyes than watch
this.

You *are* carrying your cross. It wasn't figurative. You
meant it.
The way you mean everything.

But every step you take on this sorrowful road
takes us a step further away from meaning.

Silence

Surely you can stop this. It's in your power.
We are powerless and we are scattered.
Just as you said we would be.

You and your predictions.
How we wish you could be wrong about something.

We have no words. Or if we do they die in our throats.
Our protest is silent and your protest is silence.

Only the women cry out, weeping for you.
You comfort them with more prophecy: Do not weep
for me.

They keep looking; they stay with it, for your sake.
They have the capacity.

*

A strong man is pushed forward to help you carry your
cross.
He's doing what none of us has offered to do.

Are we to make a memorial of your every stumble along
this way?
What crumbs can we pick from this table?

What bits of meaning on this meaningless way?
The kindness of that woman offering you a drink now?

We look down at our feet. The feet you washed last
night.
It made sense then. Even though you had to explain it.

But not now.
It will take an act of fantastic faith to come up with an
explanation for this.

We look down, too, because we are implicated in what
is happening.
We have played our part in this parting.

These horrors are not strokes of evil from outside our
world;
they come from our lost humanity

They spring from our silent and cowardly assent,
our failure to intervene and risk our own lives – for
yours.

We are lost – as lost as the ones taunting you,
whipping you, condemning you.

But we have to look. Even though we're far away.
Because we do love you.

And because we still hope there might be an answer to
our question:
Why is God allowing injustice to triumph over love?

Silence

The only answer we hear is hammering into your
hands –
and into our hearts.

And now they're raising you up and we can see you.
And read your lips. You are saying something.

It's hard to hear over the rolling thunder.
And the hammering, screaming and mocking in the
air.

But you take it all – all this world-noise – and you
silence it with your silence.

You are so quiet now.
Perhaps the words have run out, dear Man of Words;
Man of his Word.

The only words we catch are those of the soldiers –
doing their job,
carrying out the orders of the state.

You're saying something to them? Do we hear you
right?
You are speaking words of forgiveness:

For these soldiers, and the ones who order them to
carry out
these unforgivable acts.

And for the criminal beside you. Promising him entry
into your kingdom.
A man who has not done anything to merit it, gets to
enter before we do!

And for us.
For failing to see where this was going.

And in our defence, you offer our ignorance, our lack
of understanding.
We don't know what we're doing. Or where we're going.

How can we follow you, Lord?
Could we speak words like yours with *our* dying breath?

Still, we hang on your every breath – and hope for a
word or two more.
For even a last word from you might get us through
this.

We look up and listen but hear no consolation. No sign
except this cross.
A cross which seems to have nothing to say to anyone.

And then you say, with your one but last breath:
'It is finished.'

But what is 'it'? What did you mean, Lord? What is
finished?
Don't leave us now. Please speak.

Silence

But there is no Word.
And your silence descends like the sun.

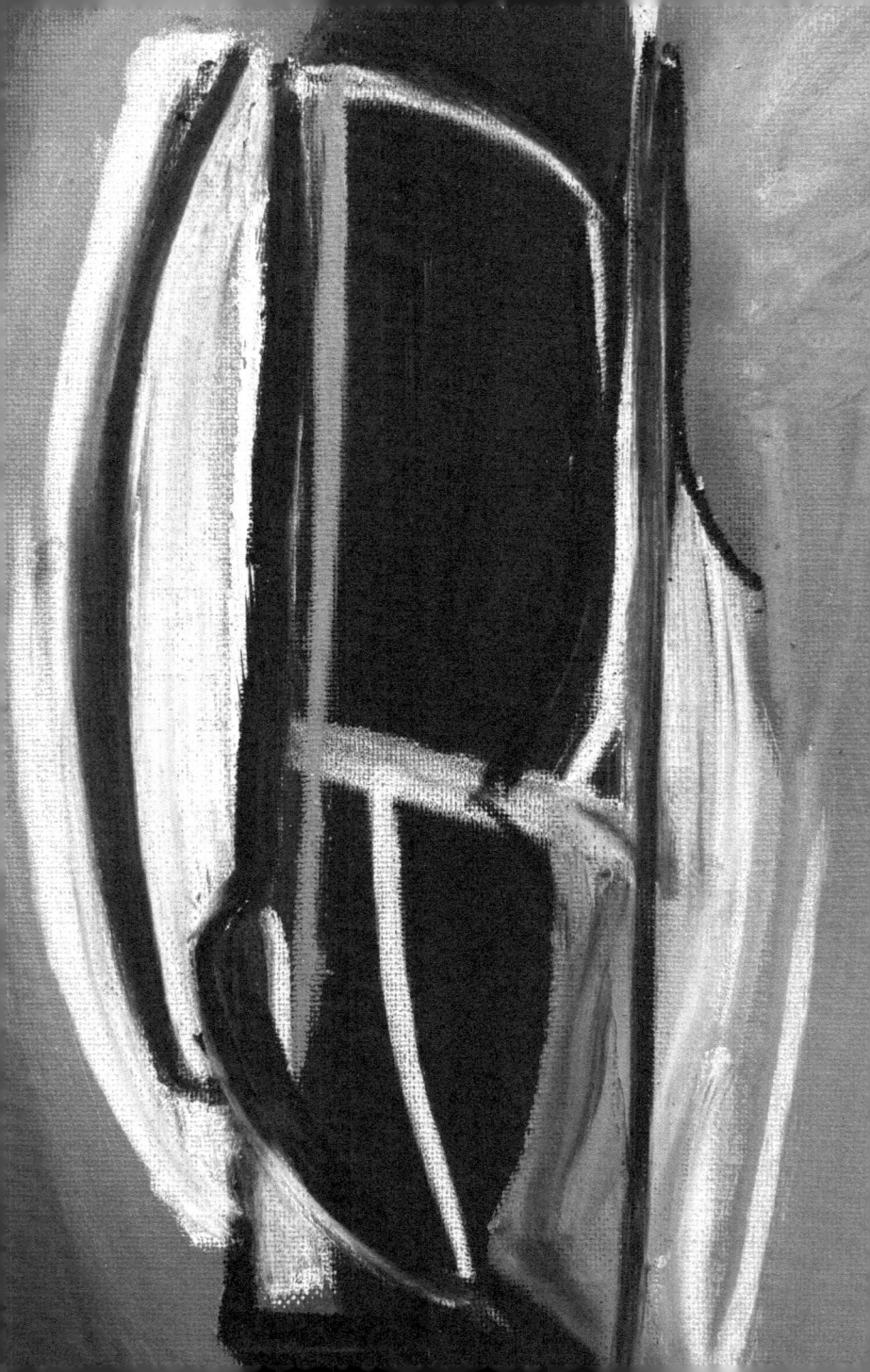

8

Execution: Good Friday

He is dead. He has reached the end of his life. And they – the fragments of his following – have reached the end of his story. They have followed him as far as they can go, and as far as he can take them. This is the end and, by any standards, it is a bad end.

Who will write about this? Who will sing about this? Who will want to tell anyone about this? This death – this execution – is an appalling spectacle. It is a crushing disappointment. A shocking failure. And, for those who love him, it will be a terrible grief to come.

They look up at his body. They don't want to, but they have nowhere else to look. Even though he has breathed his last, they half wait for a word. Something, anything, they can take with them, that might console them, help them carry on.

In the last hour, as he hung on the cross, they hung on his every word. How precious are the last words of someone we love. Every word, however muffled or whispered, has extra resonance and meaning.

What did he say? He did speak. Words of care – for his family, his friends; words of forgiveness for the criminal, for his executioners. And then, at the end, he cried out the despair of the psalm: 'My God, my God, why have you forsaken me?' And, like him, they felt the full abandonment.

In all the noise and violence and ugliness, it is hard to think. Hard to find hope and construct meaning when the subject of our love is no more. When someone we love dies, we're left with the shock and haze of grief. Like this sky, it is a black blanket shrouding all. Time slows and even seems to stop, as an indifferent world rushes on. And they wonder: are we the only ones who care?

It is finished. But what is 'it'?

Perhaps it is too soon. Too soon to extrapolate meaning from what they have witnessed. They are in shock. They should be kind to themselves. Spare themselves any exegesis while in proximity to such loss. No theological formula is going to redeem how they feel. In their need for solace, they should not freight this execution with a meaning it can't carry; stack it with sentiment, to hide the dread possibility that it means nothing more than that a good man has been unjustly killed by an unjust world.

Perhaps later, when their eyes have dried, and their vision has cleared, there will be a time to ascribe meaning to this moment. Or others in the future will be able to make sense of it. Perhaps they will write it all down. And make, at the very least, a fine eulogy out of this. But not now. Explanations and abstractions about death and the What Next don't really cut it. Death is unacceptable.

*

All they have is this unseemly execution. This cross. They have to look because that's where he is. This is where he led them and left them. If they had looked away, they might have saved themselves the pain of witnessing the suffering and the dying. If they had looked away, they might have saved themselves watching the end game of violence, and a scene of utter defeat and failure. And avoided the ridicule of having to explain why they'd been following someone whose story ends like this.

Oh, Jesus. Where did it go wrong? Was it when you raised that man from the dead and demonstrated a power that was too wonderful and too threatening for some? Or when you claimed that even the stones would praise you as you rode into Jerusalem – just six days ago? It could have been when you entered the Temple and flipped those tables. Or when you entrusted your kingdom to the likes of Judas or Peter. Or your refusal to deny your divinity in front of the very people who had the motivation to kill you for saying such things.

All of the above, and more. They wanted this story to go a different way – and there were moments when they thought they could bend it towards a happier outcome – but this is the way it's gone. This is the story they have to work with. They imagined interventions: Deus ex machina; eleventh-hour reprieves, super-heroic escapes; the sudden overthrow of oppressive power. But that is not what has happened.

Because that was not his way.

He did not become the hero they anticipated. What power he had he kept in check. If he had a superpower, it was restraint in the face of massive physical attack and psychological provocation. How did he do it? How did he not cough up a confession to his torturers, who tried to get under his skin and in his head with their taunts: 'Come on, Jesus, why don't you give sin a taste of its own medicine? Reveal your supposed divinity and start putting all this oppressive power back in its place. Strike back with that water-to-wine power, that sea-calming power, that dead-raising power.'

He had a right to defend himself. But he didn't.

They want him to come back and say something. To ask him: 'What did you mean when you said with your penultimate breath, "It is finished"?' It was hard to hear for the wailing and the whispering. They could have misheard him: '*I* am finished' would make more sense. His exhausted body was completely done.

But no, he said, '*It* is finished.' As though something had been accomplished. But what? For, as they gaze upon his spirit-emptied form, the only thing that looks finished is him. It is only death that whispers back from his still lips: 'I'm not finished, you are!'

What did you mean, Lord? 'It is finished.' What did you accomplish? Because from where they stand, it is hard to see what has been accomplished. His last words matter. They are all they have in this moment, and he never said anything that wasn't meant. So what did he mean?

They see that his suffering is finished. That the world's abuse of him, its mistreatment, its misunderstanding, its wrong answers and muddled thinking, and its treachery towards him is finished. That its constant speculation as to who he was – criminal, blasphemer, drunk, devil-possessed, rebel, prophet, false teacher, so-called Messiah – is finished. Perhaps now he can be who he really is when he returns to his Father.

Was the accomplishment he sought simply 'to die' as one of them? To accomplish a solidarity with humanity? He has done this, but they hoped for more. And his death still leaves them to face their own, alone. Without him.

Is it his mission that's finished? That is as far as they understood it: to usher in the kingdom of heaven in this land. He told them that they would continue the good work he started, and do the things he did – and more. And perhaps that is enough. Perhaps that is 'it' : to spread the good news until they too die and pass on the mantle to others. They might manage to continue for a few months. Maybe more. But without him, can they really go on?

What isn't finished – what is so crushingly clear, as the darkness descends over the land – is the domination of the world by corrupt and prideful people. For a few years, he showed unflinching resistance to violent power. He refused the opportunity just to pass by and say nothing; he confronted the self-preserving way of the world – even though he said it would kill him.

They want to believe that the sinful forces that lie behind such powers are finished. He gave it a go. He showed that worldly power can't handle any threat to its position; he exposed the connection between the collusions of the heart and the outworking of worldly powers. That the fault lines of envy and pride running through the hearts of people lead them to betray or deny or even kill the one who exposes those fault lines.

Is he the one the prophets predicted, the sacrificial lamb that cleanses us from sin? Because, from where they stand, this is hard to believe. Even this week, as a hundred thousand lambs have been slaughtered as an offering, sin holds sway. Could he be the one who 'takes upon himself the iniquity of us all'? Because from where they stand, it looks as if the iniquities of the world have defeated him. That all the sin-forces of betrayal, denial, misunderstanding, pride, greed, envy, stupidity and indifference have got dressed up in the uniforms of priests and soldiers, and even his disciples, and conspired to kill him.

Perhaps he has made a spectacle of sin and shocked some into seeing what sin does. And the shock brings awareness of our true condition. He woke many up. But did he have to die to wake us up?

Will the meaning of his words come to light later? He never said anything that did not mean something. Even as his life flashed before his eyes, he was quoting scripture, telling them something. Was he reminding them, with his last words, that all the promises and prophesies that God made are fulfilled in him. All accomplished in him?

Is that 'it'?

That he is a prophet like Moses? A champion like Joshua? A high priest like Melchizek? A king like David and Solomon, a Judah and a Joseph? Every type from the red heifer to the Temple? That he is a lamb slain? And a scapegoat not slain? A dove dipped in blood? The show bread? And the altar? The tabernacle and the mercy seat? Someone to whom all kings shall bow down? And yet one who was despised and rejected, born of a virgin? And a man without spot who meets the iniquities of us all? Someone through whom all sacrifices cease? That there is no more remembrance of sin? No more separation between us and God? That his body before us is the sacrifice, this cross the altar? That everything is summed up in him? Is that 'it'?

*

As they take his body down from the cross and take him away to be laid in the tomb, they walk with his last words turning in their minds, 'My God, my God, why have you forsaken me?' These are hard last words to hold on to. But in the pain and the grief, they can still just about remember that those words are the first of the psalm, which has a better end than this. Perhaps he was trying to get to the end of it. Or trying to tell them to keep going to the end.

As they make their sorry pilgrimage, from cross to grave, they try to finish it for him – for what it's worth. Try to get to the end of what he didn't have the breath or strength to finish himself:

Execution

All who go down to the dust will kneel before him –
those who cannot keep themselves alive.
Posterity will serve him;
future generations will be told about the Lord.
They will proclaim his righteousness,
declaring to a people yet unborn:
He has done it!

Gospel readings

Jesus before the high priest

So the soldiers, their officer, and the Jewish police arrested Jesus and bound him. First they took him to Annas, who was the father-in-law of Caiaphas, the high priest that year. Caiaphas was the one who had advised the Jews that it was better to have one person die for the people.
(John 18:12–14)

Peter denies Jesus

Simon Peter and another disciple followed Jesus. Since that disciple was known to the high priest, he went with Jesus into the courtyard of the high priest, but Peter was standing outside at the gate. So the other disciple, who was known to the high priest, went out, spoke to the woman who guarded the gate, and brought Peter in. The woman said to Peter, 'You are not also one of this man's disciples, are you?' He said, 'I am not.' Now the slaves and the police had made a charcoal fire because it was cold, and they were standing round it and warming themselves. Peter also was standing with them and warming himself.
(John 18:15–18)

The high priest questions Jesus

Then the high priest questioned Jesus about his disciples and about his teaching. Jesus answered, 'I have spoken openly to the world; I have always taught in synagogues and in the temple, where all the Jews come together. I have said nothing in secret. Why do you ask me? Ask those who

heard what I said to them; they know what I said.' When he had said this, one of the police standing nearby struck Jesus on the face, saying, 'Is that how you answer the high priest?' Jesus answered, 'If I have spoken wrongly, testify to the wrong. But if I have spoken rightly, why do you strike me?' Then Annas sent him bound to Caiaphas the high priest.
(John 18:19–24)

Peter denies Jesus again

Now Simon Peter was standing and warming himself. They asked him, 'You are not also one of his disciples, are you?' He denied it and said, 'I am not.' One of the slaves of the high priest, a relative of the man whose ear Peter had cut off, asked, 'Did I not see you in the garden with him?' Again Peter denied it, and at that moment the cock crowed.
(John 18:25–7)

Jesus before Pilate

Then they took Jesus from Caiaphas to Pilate's headquarters. It was early in the morning. They themselves did not enter the headquarters, so as to avoid ritual defilement and to be able to eat the Passover. So Pilate went out to them and said, 'What accusation do you bring against this man?' They answered, 'If this man were not a criminal, we would not have handed him over to you.' Pilate said to them, 'Take him yourselves and judge him according to your law.' The Jews replied, 'We are not permitted to put anyone to death.' (This was to fulfil what Jesus had said when he indicated the kind of death he was to die.)

Then Pilate entered the headquarters again, summoned Jesus, and asked him, 'Are you the King of the Jews?' Jesus answered, 'Do you ask this on your own, or did others tell you about me?' Pilate replied, 'I am not a Jew, am I? Your own nation and the chief priests have handed you over to me. What have you done?' Jesus answered, 'My kingdom does not belong to this world. If my kingdom belonged to this world, my followers would be fighting to keep me from being handed over to the Jews. But as it is, my kingdom is not from here.' Pilate asked him, 'So you are a king?' Jesus answered, 'You say that I am a king. For this I was born, and for this I came into the world, to testify to the truth. Everyone who belongs to the truth listens to my voice.' Pilate asked him, 'What is truth?'
(John 18:28–38)

Jesus sentenced to death

After he had said this, he went out to the Jews again and told them, 'I find no case against him. But you have a custom that I release someone for you at the Passover. Do you want me to release for you the King of the Jews?' They shouted in reply, 'Not this man but Barabbas!' Now Barabbas was a rebel.

Then Pilate took Jesus and had him flogged. And the soldiers wove a crown of thorns and put it on his head, and they dressed him in a purple robe. They kept coming up to him, saying, 'Hail, King of the Jews!' and striking him on the face. Pilate went out again and said to them, 'Look, I am bringing him out to you to let you know that I find no case against him.' So Jesus came out wearing the crown of thorns and the purple robe. Pilate said to them, 'Behold the man!' When the chief priests and the police saw him, they shouted, 'Crucify him! Crucify him!' Pilate said to them, 'Take him yourselves and crucify him; I find no case against him.' The Jews answered him, 'We have a law, and according to that law he ought to die because he has claimed to be the Son of God.'

Now when Pilate heard this, he was more afraid than ever. He entered his headquarters again and asked Jesus, 'Where are you from?' But Jesus gave him no answer. Pilate therefore said to him, 'Do you refuse to speak to me? Do you not know that I have power to release you and power to crucify you?' Jesus answered him, 'You would have no power over me unless it had been given you from above; therefore the one who handed me over to you is guilty of a greater sin.' From then on Pilate tried to release him, but the Jews cried out, 'If you release this man, you are no friend of Caesar. Everyone who claims to be a king sets himself against Caesar.'

When Pilate heard these words, he brought Jesus outside and sat on the judge's bench at a place called The Stone Pavement, or in Hebrew Gabbatha. Now it was the day of Preparation for the Passover, and it was about noon. He said to the Jews, 'Here is your King!' They cried out, 'Away with him! Away with him! Crucify him!' Pilate asked them, 'Shall I crucify your King?' The chief priests answered, 'We have no king but Caesar.' Then he handed him over to them to be crucified.

(John 18:38 – 19.16)

The crucifixion of Jesus

So they took Jesus, and carrying the cross by himself he went out to what is called the Place of the Skull, which in Hebrew is called Golgotha. There they crucified him and with him two others, one on either side, with Jesus between them. Pilate also had an inscription written and put on the cross. It read, 'Jesus of Nazareth, the King of the Jews.' Many of the Jews read this inscription because the place where Jesus was crucified was near the city, and it was written in Hebrew, in Latin, and in Greek. Then the chief priests of the Jews said to Pilate, 'Do not write, "The King of the Jews", but, "This man said, I am King of the Jews."' Pilate answered, 'What I have written I have written.' When the soldiers had crucified Jesus, they took his clothes and divided them into four parts, one for each soldier. They also took his tunic; now the tunic was seamless, woven in one piece from the top. So they said to one another, 'Let us not tear it but cast lots for it to see who will get it.' This was to fulfil what the scripture says,

'They divided my clothes among themselves,
   and for my clothing they cast lots.'

And that is what the soldiers did.

Meanwhile, standing near the cross of Jesus were his mother, and his mother's sister, Mary the wife of Clopas, and Mary Magdalene. When Jesus saw his mother and the disciple whom he loved standing beside her, he said to his mother, 'Woman, here is your son.' Then he said to the disciple, 'Here is your mother.' And from that hour the disciple took her into his own home.

After this, when Jesus knew that all was now finished, he said (in order to fulfil the scripture), 'I am thirsty.' A jar full of sour wine was standing there. So they put a sponge full of the wine on a branch of hyssop and held it to his mouth. When Jesus had received the wine, he said, 'It is finished.' Then he bowed his head and gave up his spirit.

(John 19:16–30)

Questions

- Imagine you too are present at this execution; where would you be standing and why?
- What do you think is 'accomplished' or 'finished' on the cross?
- Can you think of an example in your own life where you have had to die to something?

9

Encounter: Easter

The day I sat down to write this Easter reflection, I received the news that my mum had died. I tried to get this Holy Week story to its extraordinary end, but I couldn't do it. I couldn't think straight. I was blinded by a powerful grief. I momentarily forgot what happens next. I was stuck in Good Friday, and Jesus was still on the cross. The end.

I decided that I'd leave Jesus there for now, and return to him later. He wasn't going anywhere. I'd come back, when I could stop crying, and maybe string a few sentences together; write something that might be a help to others, or even to me. So, I put down my pen, left him on the cross and went for a walk.

As I walked, I thought about my mum. I couldn't believe that I wouldn't see or talk to her again; that this was the end of her story. I had hoped to see her that week. But the loss – the utter finality – had to be faced. She was not here any more. I would not see her again. Death is an end. For her, for me, for all of us.

In my mind, I was walking to Emmaus, the village about seven miles from Jerusalem, like those two downcast travellers, who had witnessed the death of Jesus and with it the death of their hopes. They too were grieving the loss of someone they loved, someone utterly essential to their lives and whom they could not imagine being without.

In the gospel story, Jesus pulls up alongside them, as they are walking, and they don't recognise him. Why would they? He's meant to be dead. And they are in shock, with their heads down and their hearts low. They were trying to make sense of what had happened, in a tumultuous week that had ended, so painfully, with the death of this person they loved.

They tell the traveller about the sad events in Jerusalem and mention a rumour that some women claimed to have seen Jesus alive at the sepulchre. Although when they went to the tomb, they found no evidence of his presence.

The traveller walks with the two disciples on the road. And, as they go, he suggests that this man, whom they loved so much, sounds very much like the one prophesied in scripture. The one who would suffer and die, and then rise again. As they walk, he starts to walk them through the scriptures, pointing to where these things are said. And then suggests to them that the one they are mourning must be the one the prophets foretold.

When they reach Emmaus, the two travellers invite this stranger to have supper with them and, just as they break the bread, they suddenly recognise who it is who's been walking with them all this time. It is Jesus, risen to life.

As I walked from Good Friday – head bowed in grief – I felt that same presence, gently walking me through the story, coaxing me back to remembering how it goes. At first it goes to the darkest place we can go – to death – but then it emerges in an encounter, not with an abstract idea but with a person. From cross to grave, from grave to a risen Christ.

This encounter reminds us what it is that we hope for, and who it is we hope in. It reminds us that Jesus himself promised that he would not leave us as orphans; that he would be raised to life, and will remain with us.

The gospel is sad news before it is glad news. And the good news comes at a cost. Death is an end. But not The End. It takes the risen Christ to explain and give meaning to what happened – back there on the cross. It requires a resurrected Jesus to helps us make sense of loss, and to tell us that death does not have the last word in this life. To transform this story into something unexpected. Make it a beginning, rather than the thing we feared it might be: The End.

It may be that you have missed the events of these last few days. And that you are here just in time to hear this good news. You have been spared the confrontations, the betrayals and trials, and a terrible death. You have not had to think about the detail of all that has come to pass, from the moment Jesus arrived in Jerusalem on Palm Sunday to his final words on the cross, and his broken body being taken to the tomb, and the disciples broken and scattered and not sure what to do next.

But that doesn't matter. If you are here for the good news, the good news is that the last get to be first anyway.

The joy of this story is that the risen Christ meets us at whatever point in our own journey we have got to. And that we join his story at any point in time.

His very presence is the answer to the impossible questions that we have. He is a pilgrim walking with us on the road, transforming our despair and disappointment, and setting our hearts on fire with hope. Confirming us in our faith and empowering us to follow him.

He encounters us with the reality that death is not the end, for him, for you, for me and for the ones we love. The risen Christ finishes the psalm he started crying on the cross and ends with the astounding news: 'He has done it.'

He is risen, indeed!

Gospel reading

The walk to Emmaus

Now on that same day two of them were going to a village called Emmaus, about seven miles from Jerusalem, and talking with each other about all these things that had happened. While they were talking and discussing, Jesus himself came near and went with them, but their eyes were kept from recognizing him. And he said to them, 'What are you discussing with each other while you walk along?' They stood still, looking sad. Then one of them, whose name was Cleopas, answered him, 'Are you the only stranger in Jerusalem who does not know the things that have taken place there in these days?' He asked them, 'What things?' They replied, 'The things about Jesus of Nazareth, who was a prophet mighty in deed and word before God and all the people, and how our chief priests and leaders handed him over to be condemned to death and crucified him. But we had hoped that he was the one to redeem Israel. Yes, and besides all this, it is now the third day since these things took place. Moreover, some women of our group astounded us. They were at the tomb early this morning, and when they did not find his body there they came back and told us that they had indeed seen a vision of angels who said that he was alive. Some of those who were with us went to the tomb and found it just as the women had said, but they did not see him.' Then he said to them, 'Oh, how foolish you are and how slow of heart to believe all that the prophets have declared! Was it not necessary that the Messiah should suffer these things and then enter into his glory?' Then beginning with Moses and all the prophets, he interpreted to them the things about himself in all the scriptures. As they came near the village to which they were going, he walked ahead as if he were going on. But they urged him strongly, saying, 'Stay with us, because it is almost evening and the day is now nearly over.' So he went in to stay with them. When he was at the table with them, he took bread, blessed and broke it, and gave it to them. Then their eyes were opened, and they recognized him, and he vanished from their sight. They said to each other, 'Were not our hearts burning within us while he was talking to us on the road, while he was opening the scriptures to us?' That same hour they got up and returned to Jerusalem, and they found the eleven and their companions gathered together. They were saying, 'The Lord has risen indeed, and he has appeared to Simon!' Then they told what had happened on the road and how he had been made known to them in the breaking of the bread.

(Luke 24:13–35)

Questions

- Have you had an 'Emmaus moment' – an encounter with Jesus? Can you describe it?
- Do you think the crucifixion is more important for the Christian message than the resurrection? Which do you think about more?
- In your experience, in what ways does it makes sense to say that 'Jesus is alive'?

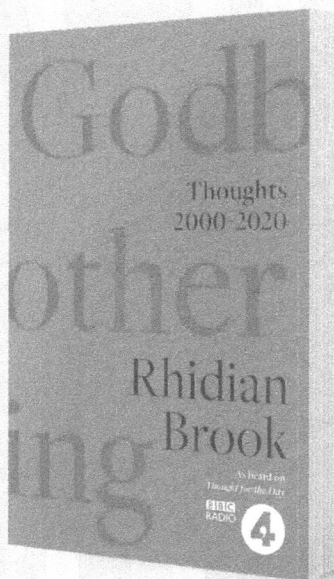